C000071717

IMAGES OF THE
NORTH NORFOLK COAST

Photographed by John Curtis

SALMON

INTRODUCTION

The wide open skies and unspoilt nature of the North Norfolk coast draw many visitors to this beautiful and remote area, which exudes a timeless beauty and offers a more leisurely pace of life. Here, where the North Sea meets the shore, there are miles of wide, sandy beaches, little harbours where boats moor, and cliff tops with panoramic views. With some ninety miles of coastline, the county of Norfolk is almost an island, cut off from Suffolk by the River Waveney and the Little Ouse, and from Cambridgeshire by the Great Ouse and the River Nene.

Over the centuries, many changes have occurred along this coast. In some places, the silting up of rivers has lead to once important ports now being land locked, while in other areas, erosion has caused whole streets and houses to fall into the sea. The coastline is under constant attack from the powerful waves of the North Sea, due to its exposed position, and flooding is a persistent threat. Submerged beneath the waves off the coast of Norfolk lies the remnants of an ancient forest which once stretched far out into what is now open sea. During and after the last Ice Age, a massive land bridge, known now as Doggerland, connected East Anglia to the Netherlands, Germany and Denmark, and fossilised bits of wood still appear in many places along the coast at low tide.

This, the Land of the North Folk was once part of the Kingdom of East Anglia, ruled by the Anglo-Saxons after the Romans left.

East Beach, Cromer

By the time of the Domesday Book, Norfolk was one of the country's most populated areas; however, the Black Death of 1349–1350 and further outbreaks of plagues over the centuries reduced numbers significantly.

The Middle Ages saw the growth of the wool trade with export to northern Europe giving rise to large ports, particularly at Blakeney Haven and Cley. This wealth is reflected in the many impressive churches which were rebuilt in the 14th and 15th centuries, such as those at Salthouse and Wiveton.

The agricultural revolution of the 18th century later brought prosperity to Norfolk, while the many fishing villages and towns on the north coast supported fishermen who brought home their catch from the North Sea. The herring industry grew significantly, and many boats were built locally with shipyards expanding in the larger towns.

Fishing remains an important, if considerably scaled down, industry, with small fishing fleets working off the coast, catching mainly crab and lobster, but also bass, tope and cod.

Tourism came late to Norfolk as it was one of the last counties to benefit from the growing railway network. Cromer and Sheringham were first developed as holiday resorts by the late Victorians, and over the years, the delights of the North Norfolk coast and its many lovely little villages and towns have attracted increasing numbers of visitors, including many artists and writers.

Salt marshes, dunes and intertidal flats give the North Norfolk coast its distinctive character. So unspoilt and remarkable is this magnificent stretch of coastline that much of it has been designated an Area of Outstanding Natural Beauty and large parts of the coastal marshlands have been given over to nature reserves. Off the coast are sandbanks so rich in nutrients for birds and fish life that they have been designated as Marine Protection Zones.

Wells-next-the-Sea

Hunstanton Cliffs

The remarkable layered cliffs at Hunstanton, which consist of reddish limestone topped by a white chalk layer, provide a perfect nesting site for a wide variety of seabirds. The beach is a magnet for fossil hunters, and at low tide, the weathered remains of the steam trawler *Sheraton*, which ran aground here in 1947, make a reappearance.

Norfolk Lavender, Heacham

Heacham lies in a pleasant rural situation overlooking The Wash and is known as the centre of the Norfolk lavender-growing industry. In midsummer, the fields are ablaze with rich shades of mauve and purple, and the scent of lavender fills the air as it is picked and distilled to produce perfume and other products.

Thornham Creek

Until Hunstanton developed as the major port in the area, Thornham had a flourishing coastal trade. It is situated on a natural creek which is still well used by fishing boats in search of the crabs, cockles and mussels which are found in the mudflats. The village boasts several old inns and an interesting church, surrounded by ilex trees, which contains a fine 15th century screen and font as well as some noteworthy carved bench ends.

Old Hunstanton Beach

Hunstanton is popular for its wide sandy beaches and the many rock pools which form below the cliffs at low tide. The beach at Old Hunstanton lies within view of the lighthouse and the ruins of St. Edmund's Chapel which dates back to 1272. It is perfect for long tranquil walks and is also popular with kite surfers.

Brancaster Staithe
Two miles away from the village, Brancaster Staithe stands on a creek which opens into Brancaster harbour. Almost landlocked on the edge of the marshes, it is a popular yachting centre and from here it is possible to visit the bird sanctuary and National Nature Reserve of Scolt Head Island.

Brancaster Beach
Originally a Roman fortress built about AD 300 as part of the coastal defences, Brancaster is a quiet little resort with a handsome church. Salt marshes and sandy dunes planted with marram grass, to hold up the process of erosion, separate the village from its lovely sandy beach which is backed by a massive sea wall.

Burnham Overy

Between Brancaster and Holkham lies the delightful village of Burnham Overy, one of several villages in the area, known collectively as The Burnhams. A fine restored tower mill has been converted into a private house and stands on the edge of the little village, across the road from the remains of a Carmelite friary.

Burnham Overy Staithe

The silting up of the River Burn prevented sailing craft from reaching Burnham Overy and led to the establishment of the Staithe a mile downstream. Although it was once a busy little port, like similar havens on this coast, it is today linked to the sea only by a sandy creek running between saltings.

Church of St. Margaret, Burnham Norton
The church at Burnham Norton is dedicated to
St. Margaret of Antioch and has one of the most
complete round towers in Norfolk, built between
1000 and 1066. Set in a superb position on a
hilltop, this beautiful church is noted for its
heptagonal 'wineglass' pulpit, which has six
painted panels and dates from 1450.

Church of All Saints, Burnham Thorpe
The tiny 13th century Church of All Saints at
Burnham Thorpe holds much memorabilia to
Admiral Lord Nelson whose father was the
parson here. Born in the village and baptised in
the church, Nelson returned to live at the
parsonage for a time after his early years in the
Navy, but is buried at St. Paul's Cathedral.

The Green, Burnham Market

This beautiful village is centred round a delightful village green which is surrounded by many fine buildings dating from the 17th and 18th centuries. In the centre stands a memorial cross commemorating the fallen in the two World Wars. The rise in popularity of the village, with its many little shops and eateries giving it a lovely cosmopolitan feel, has given rise to the nickname 'Chelsea on Sea'.

Burnham Market

The largest of the Burnhams, thought to once have been a centre for the amber trade, Burnham Market grew from three separate villages, Burnham Sutton, Burnham Ulph and Burnham Westgate. With the coming of the railway, a station was built here in 1866, and the railway company gave it the name of Burnham Market.

Abbey Church of St. Mary, North Creake

The ruins of an early 13th century abbey of Augustinian priors lies to the north of the village of North Creake alongside the River Burn. In 1508, the plague killed its inhabitants and the church was left abandoned. Later the land and buildings were passed to Christ's College, Cambridge.

Church of St. Mary, South Creake

Dating in part from the 12th century, the impressive Church of St. Mary, at South Creake, is one of only a few Norfolk churches to have a seven-sacrament font. Extensive rebuilding in the 15th century saw the hammer-beam roof added which has beautiful carved angels resting on the wall posts.

Walsingham Priory

All that remains of the Augustinian Priory which was built around the replica of the Holy House of Nazareth is the east wall and the impressive east window. Dating from the 13th century, it stands in the Priory Gardens, its towering twin turrets resplendent with knapped flintwork panels.

Shrine of Our Lady, Little Walsingham

The Anglican Shrine was built to house the statue of Our Lady of Walsingham and also holds a replica of the Holy House. It was created in the 1930s from derelict farm buildings and cottages, close to the ruins of the original medieval priory.

Slipper Chapel, Houghton St. Giles
Legend has it that pilgrims travelling to visit the medieval shrine at Walsingham would remove their shoes at Houghton St. Giles and complete the last mile of the journey barefoot, thus giving the Slipper Chapel its name. Dedicated to St. Catherine of Alexandria, the chapel was built during the mid-14th century when Walsingham was second only to Canterbury in importance for pilgrims coming to England.

Common Place, Little Walsingham
This beautiful village, set amidst parks and woodland, boasts many fine medieval and Georgian buildings, notably those grouped around the medieval village well with its 16th century octagonal pump house. Once the only street lighting in the village, an iron brazier sits on the roof and is known as 'The Beacon'.

Holkham Hall

One of the finest Palladian mansions in the country, Holkham Hall was built between 1734 and 1759 for the Coke family. Known for its superb Marble Hall and Statue Gallery, the magnificent house stands in a beautiful park, landscaped by William Kent, near a lake which was originally an inlet from the sea.

Holkham Beach

The impressive expanse of glorious, golden sands and wide, open skies bring visitors from near and far to the North Norfolk coast. Two miles west of Wells-next-the-Sea is Holkham Bay, which lies at the centre of an important National Nature Reserve, stretching from Burnham Norton to Blakeney.

The Quay, Wells-next-the-Sea
Wells-next-the-Sea has long been dependent on the sea for its trade and it remains so today, although the town is now some way from open water. The quay is dominated by an old granary building, with its distinctive overhanging gantry. Built in 1903, it is a reminder of the malting industry which once thrived here.

Beach Huts, Wells-next-the-Sea
The beach can be reached from the town by a road along the western side of the harbour channel and also by a miniature railway. It lies almost a mile further out and is lined with a row of colourful beach huts. These pretty wooden huts have become increasingly popular over the years and each has its own unique appeal.

The Buttlands, Wells-next-the-Sea
Usually the name Buttlands derives from the use of an area for archery practice, but here at Wells it refers to the area which was once a 'wasteland'. It is the town's open space, lined with mature trees and surrounded by stately early 19th century houses and two public houses – the Crown Hotel and the Globe Inn.

The Harbour, Wells-next-the-Sea
The colourful harbour is now the permanent home of *The Albatros*, a one-hundred-year-old Dutch clipper, which was built in Rotterdam in 1899. During the Second World War, the cargo ship was used by the Danish Resistance, and later, in the 1990s, it carried soya beans from Belgium to the harbour at Wells.

Church of St. John the Baptist, Stiffkey
Nestling in a valley next to a river of the same name, the coastal village of Stiffkey is four miles east of Wells-next-the-Sea. St. John's sits on a prominent spur above the river and is one of two churches which once stood on this ancient site. Built mainly in the Perpendicular style, it presents an attractive mixture of flint work, dressed stone and old red bricks.

Binham Priory
The ruins of this Benedictine house, which was founded in the 11th century, stand surrounded by farmland mid-way between Blakeney and Great Walsingham. The Norman nave is now used as the parish church, and the splendid west front which was built of Barnack stone and local flint between 1226 and 1244 is one of the finest remaining examples of Early English architecture.

Blakeney from Morston Quay
A lane leads down from the little village of
Morston to a tidal creek where The National
Trust owns an extensive stretch of the marshes
together with Morston Quay. It is a popular area
with bird-watchers and walkers, and offers
beautiful views over the marshes towards
Blakeney further inland.

Glandford
Set in the valley of the River Glaven, the little
hamlet of Glandford has some charming flint
and red brick cottages. Crossing the river next
to the old ford, a footbridge leads into the water
meadows from where there are pretty views of
St. Martin's Church, which was completely
rebuilt in the 19th century.

The Quay, Blakeney

One of the most enchanting of North Norfolk's coastal village, is Blakeney, once a busy commercial medieval port until the estuary silted up. The last working port on the Glaven estuary, its popular quay is today a fine boating centre, and from here, there are fine views out over the marshes towards the sea. Blakeney is set on a small hill and its narrow roads are lined with traditional cottages of local flint, many of which are painted in bright colours. In a prominent position on the quay sits the Blakeney Hotel, opened in 1923 and built on the site of an old inn, which was a notorious smugglers' haunt.

Blakeney Point
Established since 1912, the nature reserve at Blakeney Point was the first to be set up in Norfolk. There is an important seal sanctuary here, where there is a flourishing colony of common seals. Grey seals can also be seen basking on the sand bars. The Point is a popular nesting site for a wide variety of birds.

Church of St. Nicholas, Blakeney
The tower of St. Nicholas's Church is a prominent local landmark, and the turret on the north-east end of the chancel houses a beacon light. The chancel itself, dating from 1220, is an outstanding example of the Early English style. There is a superb hammer-beam roof in the nave and much beautiful woodwork throughout.

Cley-next-the-Sea
The beautiful windmill at Cley-next-the-Sea dates from 1850 but has long since stopped grinding corn. It is the best-known feature of this once important wool trading port, which during medieval times was greater than King's Lynn, The mill looks particularly picturesque seen across the Cley Marshes and the River Glaven.

Newgate Green, Cley-next-the-Sea
Shipping quays once lined both sides of the River Glaven at Cley-next-the-Sea where ships of considerable size docked at Newgate Green on the southern edge of the village. However, today, the large cruciform church of St. Margaret by the Green looks out over pretty flint cottages as the sea is now more than half a mile away.

Cley Marshes

One of the country's finest bird-watching sites, Cley Marshes Nature Reserve lies to the north-east of the village towards the sea and is a haven for a variety of different birds species. Boardwalks offer a chance to get close to the wildlife here and a new visitor centre, built to a cutting edge design, has recently opened.

Salthouse

Until the fens were reclaimed in 1637, Salthouse was a small port with access to the sea through the Salthouse Mayne Channel. Sitting on high ground above the salt marshes, the impressive Church of St. Nicholas was built at the turn of the 16th century by Sir Henry Heydon whose wife was related to Anne Boleyn.

Holt

Founded at the crossing point of two major routes, the pretty market town of Holt suffered a devastating fire in 1708 which destroyed the majority of its buildings. It was subsequently rebuilt around its market place and so the architectural style of the town reflects Georgian and later periods. Surrounded by well-wooded parks, it is popular for its wealth of little shops, cafés and galleries, but perhaps best known for its famous school, Gresham's, which was founded in 1555.

Letheringsett Mill

The last remaining water mill to produce flour in Norfolk, Letheringsett Mill dates from 1802 and stands in the Glaven Valley just east of Holt. The red brick structure we see today is the latest in a succession of mills on this site, which is mentioned in the Domesday Book as 'Leringaseta'.

The Cross, Holt

This fine cross of Clipsham stone stands in the Market Place at the centre of Holt, commemorating fallen heroes. It was designed by the architect, H.H. Palmer, and unveiled in 1921. Holt is the western terminus for the North Norfolk Railway, or Poppy Line, which takes passengers on a round trip through the Norfolk countryside by steam train.

Priory and Church of All Saints, Weybourne

All Saints' Church at Weybourne, which is surrounded by the ruins of a major Augustinian priory, dates from the 11th century, but the handsome porch of brick-and-flint chequer work was added some four hundred years later. Below Kelling Heath, the church stands on the site of an earlier cruciform church and has an interesting off-centred chancel arch.

Weybourne Beach

Midway between Cley and Sheringham is the village of Weybourne with its steep shingle beach and deep inshore water. Now it is popular with fishermen, but at one time, it provided such a threat from invading fleets that in 1588 it was garrisoned against the Armada.

Weybourne Mill

Built in 1850, picturesque Weybourne Mill is a five-storey red brick tower mill which stands in an enviable position beside the coast road to Blakeney. It ceased working around 1916 and is today a private residence with unrivalled sea views.

Sheringham Cliffs

The beach below the soft chalk cliffs at Sheringham is a popular hunting ground for fossil collectors. Hidden out at sea some seventeen kilometres off the coast, the new Sheringham Shoal Offshore Wind Farm will provide enough electricity to supply the North Norfolk coast twice over.

Sheringham Park

A personal favourite of landscape gardener Humphry Repton, who designed the layout, Sheringham Park is famous for its collection of rhododendrons, azaleas, magnolias and camellias. The hill-top temple was part of Repton's original plans, but it was not completed until 1975 to a design by James Fletcher-Watson.

The Beach, Sheringham

Well known for its colourful crab boats, Sheringham became popular with holiday-makers after the arrival of the railway in 1887. As the resort lacks a natural harbour, the beach, which is comprised of shingle and gently sloping sand, provides a safe resting place for the boats when they are not at sea. The beach is backed by a promenade which extends all the way along the sea front.

Fishermen's Slope, Sheringham

Below the promenade is Fishermen's Slope which provides access to the beach where the crab boats are drawn up. The small fishing fleet here brings in lobster and the famous Cromer Crab, which is a favourite treat for seafood lovers due to its particularly sweet meat. The boathouse at the top of the slope houses the *Henry Ramey Upcher*, an old lifeboat which served the town up until 1935.

East Runton Beach

Between Sheringham and Cromer are the twin villages of West and East Runton – the Runtons, as they are collectively known. Once a small fishing village, East Runton became a popular caravan holiday destination in the 1950s. Its wide sandy beach is backed by low crumbling cliffs, and attracts families and surfers.

West Runton Beach

The beach at West Runton occurs in one of the few gaps in the cliffs along this stretch of the coast. The soft cliffs are home to several rare species of beetle and invertebrates not found anywhere else. Fossils are regularly exposed during the natural erosion of the cliffs; most famously the skeleton of a woolly mammoth.

The Beach, Cromer

Originally a small fishing village, Cromer developed into the principal resort on the North Norfolk coast, known for its fine beaches, cliff scenery and invigorating climate. A massive sea wall, built to prevent encroachment by the sea, provides access to the beach from the promenade which extends the length of the seafront.

Cromer Pier

Reaching 450 feet into the sea, Cromer's splendid pier was opened in 1901 and it was erected after an earlier wooden structure had been destroyed by the high seas. At the end of the pier is the famous Pavilion Theatre and the Lifeboat House, originally built in 1923 but recently replaced.

HENRY BLOGG
G.C. B.E.M.
COXSWAIN OF CROMER
LIFE-BOATS 1909-1947
WINNER OF THE R.N.L.I.
GOLD MEDAL
FOR CONSPICUOUS
GALLANTRY 3 TIMES
OF ITS SILVER MEDAL
4 TIMES
WITH THE HELP OF
HIS GALLANT CREW
RESCUED 873 LIVES
DURING 53 YEARS
OF SERVICE
-ONE OF THE
BRAVEST MEN
WHO EVER LIVED
DIED JUNE 13TH 1954

Henry Blogg Memorial, Cromer

A bronze bust of the famous lifeboatman Henry Blogg looks out over the North Sea from its position on Cromer's sea front. It honours his many years of dedicated service on the Cromer lifeboat, for which he received three gold and four silver medals as well as the George Cross and the British Empire medal.

Lifeboat Museum, Cromer

Opened in 2006, the Lifeboat Museum tells the story of the local lifeboat crew and in particular of Henry Blogg, whose medals can been see as part of the exhibition. The centre of the museum is a Watson class lifeboat, the *HF Bailey*, which dates from 1935 and served under Blogg during the Second World War.

Cromer Lighthouse

In the 1660s, many new applications were made to erect lighthouses around the British coast and in 1669 a tower was erected at Cromer. The ever-encroaching sea eventually claimed the original lighthouse, and the present beacon, a fine white octagonal tower standing about half a mile from the cliff edge, was built in 1833.

Felbrigg Hall

Standing in a large park just south of Cromer, Felbrigg Hall is a well-preserved Jacobean mansion containing original 18th century furniture and pictures. The estate covers some 1,760 acres of parkland and woodland, and its formal gardens include a delightful walled garden with a picturesque octagonal dovecote.

Overstrand Beach

Once popular with the rich and famous after the romantic tales of writer, Clement Scott, drew people to the village, the quiet resort of Overstrand has a gently sloping beach of good firm sand. It is reached by steps or winding paths down the lofty cliffs, and a ramp enables fishing boats to be drawn down to the shore.

Church of St. John the Baptist's Head, Trimingham

A small village on the coast road between Cromer and Mundesley, Trimingham is situated on one of the highest parts of the Norfolk coast. Its ancient church received its unusual dedication in medieval times, when a life-sized alabaster head of the saint was kept here.

Poppyland, Overstrand

The term 'Poppyland' was first coined by Clement Scott, a London playwright and travel writer, who came to the area in the 1880s. The county flower of Norfolk, the bright red poppy was known as the 'corn rose' in medieval times, and during the First World War, it became the international symbol of remembrance.

Church of St. Michael, Sidestrand

Coastal erosion forced the rebuilding further inland of St. Michael's Church in 1881. The original for many years clung onto the cliffs, until in 1916, it finally disappeared over the cliff edge. Clement Scott romanticised the old church and churchyard in the verse, 'The Garden of Sleep'. The church has a round tower topped by a tall octagonal stage.

Stow Mill

A little way to the south of the village of Mundesley, in the parish of Paston, stands Stow Mill, a fine black-painted tower mill complete with sails and restored cap and fanwheel. It was built between 1825 and 1827 by James Haze and last worked in the early 1900s when it was converted into a dwelling.

Published in Great Britain by J. Salmon Ltd.,
Sevenoaks, Kent TN13 1BB.
Telephone 01732 452381 Email enquiries@jsalmon.co.uk

Design by John Curtis.
Photographs © John Curtis. All rights reserved.
No part of this book may be produced, stored in a retrieval
system or transmitted in any form or by any means
without prior written permission of the publishers.

ISBN 978-1-84640-297-5

Printed in China.

Title page photograph: Morston Quay
Front cover photograph: Cley-next-the-Sea
Back cover photograph: Cromer
First Edition 2008 Revised Edition 2011

Salmon Books
ENGLISH IMAGES SERIES
Photography by John Curtis

Titles available in this series

English Abbeys and Priories

English Gardens

English Country Towns

English Cottages

English Landscape Gardens

English Follies

English Villages

English Country Pubs

English Castles

English Cathedrals

English Country Churches

Jane Austen's England

Romantic England

Mysterious England